My Canada
NEW BRUNSWICK

By Sheila Yazdani

TABLE OF CONTENTS

New Brunswick 3

Glossary 22

Index 24

A Crabtree Seedlings Book

Crabtree Publishing
crabtreebooks.com

School-to-Home Support for Caregivers and Teachers

This book helps children grow by letting them practice reading. Here are a few guiding questions to help the reader build his or her comprehension skills. Possible answers appear in red.

Before Reading:
- What do I know about New Brunswick?
  - *I know that New Brunswick is a province.*
  - *I know that New Brunswick has a lot of rivers.*

- What do I want to learn about New Brunswick?
  - *I want to learn which famous people were born in New Brunswick.*
  - *I want to learn what the provincial flag looks like.*

During Reading:
- What have I learned so far?
  - *I have learned that Fredericton is the capital of New Brunswick.*
  - *I have learned that the rocks at Hopewell Rocks Provincial Park are up to 21 meters (70 feet) tall.*

- I wonder why…
  - *I wonder why the provincial flower is the purple violet.*
  - *I wonder why there are many river lighthouses in New Brunswick.*

After Reading:
- What did I learn about New Brunswick?
  - *I have learned that you can explore St. Martins Sea Caves.*
  - *I have learned that the provincial bird is the black-capped chickadee.*

- Read the book again and look for the glossary words.
  - *I see the word **capital** on page 6, and the word **kayaking** on page 14. The other glossary words are found on pages 22 and 23.*

I live in Saint John. It is on the shore of the Bay of Fundy.

The Saint John City Market is the oldest farmers' market in Canada!

New Brunswick is a **province** in eastern Canada. The **capital** is Fredericton.

Fun Fact: Moncton is the largest city in New Brunswick.

The provincial bird is the black-capped chickadee.

Fun Fact: About 16,400 metric tons (18,000 tons) of lobster are caught in New Brunswick each year.

My provincial flag is red and yellow. It has a lion and a ship on it.

There are many river **lighthouses** in New Brunswick.

I enjoy visiting Hopewell Rocks Provincial Park. I like to go **kayaking** around the big rocks.

Fun Fact: The rocks are up to 21 meters (70 feet) tall!

It is fun to tour Campobello Island.

Actor Donald Sutherland was born in New Brunswick. Former NHL hockey player Rick Bowness was also born in New Brunswick.

Fun Fact: George Edwin King, a former **justice** of the Supreme Court of Canada, was born in Saint John, New Brunswick.

I like to explore St. Martins **Sea Caves**.

Glossary

capital (CAP-ih-tuhl): The city or town where the government of a country, state, or province is located

justice (JUST-iss): A judge

kayaking (KIE-yak-ing): A watersport that uses a long, narrow boat that is pointed at both ends

lighthouse (LIET-hows): A tower with a strong light that is used to guide ships

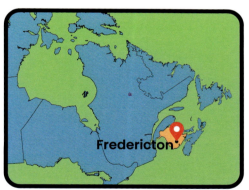

province (PROV-ins): One of the large areas that some countries, such as Canada, are divided into

sea caves (see kayvz): Caves that are formed in cliffs by the wave action of the sea

Index

black-capped chickadee 8
Campobello Island 17
Fredericton 6
lobster 10, 11
Saint John 4, 5, 19
Sutherland, Donald 18

About the Author

Sheila Yazdani lives in Ontario near Niagara Falls with her dog Daisy. She likes to travel across Canada to learn about its history, people, and landscape. She loves to cook new dishes she learns about. Her favorite treat is Nanaimo bars.

Written by: Sheila Yazdani
Designed and Illustrated by: Bobbie Houser
Series Development: James Earley
Proofreader: Melissa Boyce
Educational Consultant: Marie Lemke M.Ed.

Photographs:
Alamy: Naturfoto-Online: p. 16; History and Art Collection: p. 19, 22; Dave G. Houser: p. 20
Newscom: Douglas R. Clifford/ZUMA Press: p. 18 right
Shutterstock: Paul Reeves Photography: cover; Cindy Creighton: p. 3; gvictoria: p. 4; RozenskiP: p. 5; Media Guru: p. 6, 22-23; Adwo: p. 7; sebartz: p. 8; gresei: p. 9; k-photography_113: p. 10-11; spwidoff: p. 11; Millenius: p. 12; gvictoria: p. 13, 21, 23; Alberto Loyo: p. 14-15, 22; Ken Morris: p. 15; Russ Heinl: p. 17; DFree: p. 18 left

Crabtree Publishing

crabtreebooks.com   800-387-7650
Copyright © 2025 Crabtree Publishing
All rights reserved. No part of this publication may be reproduced, stored in a retrieval system or be transmitted in any form or by any means, electronic, mechanical, photocopying, recording, or otherwise, without the prior written permission of Crabtree Publishing. In Canada: We acknowledge the financial support of the Government of Canada through the Canada Book Fund for our publishing activities.

Printed in Canada/012024/CP20231127

Published in Canada
Crabtree Publishing
616 Welland Avenue
St. Catharines, Ontario
L2M 5V6

Published in the United States
Crabtree Publishing
347 Fifth Avenue
Suite 1402-145
New York, New York, 10016

Library and Archives Canada Cataloguing in Publication
Available at Library and Archives Canada

Library of Congress Cataloging-in-Publication Data
Available at the Library of Congress

Hardcover: 978-1-0398-3854-3
Paperback: 978-1-0398-3939-7
Ebook (pdf): 978-1-0398-4020-1
Epub: 978-1-0398-4092-8